EDGE BOOKS

GROSS

GROSS SCIENCE PROJECTS

GUIDES

by Jodi Lyn Wheeler-Toppen

Consultant:
Dr. Jon E. Ahlquist, Associate Professor
Dept. of Earth, Ocean, and Atmospheric Science
Florida State University
Tallahassee, Florida

CAPSTONE PRESS
a capstone imprint

Edge Books are published by Capstone Press,
1710 Roe Crest Drive, North Mankato, Minnesota 56003
www.capstonepub.com

Library of Congress Cataloging-in-Publication Data
Wheeler-Toppen, Jodi.
Gross science projects / by Jodi Lyn Wheeler-Toppen.
pcm.—(Edge books. Gross guides)
Summary: "Describes fun, gross science projects in a step-by-step format"
—Provided by publisher.
Includes bibliographical references and index.
ISBN 978-1-4296-9924-2 (library binding)
ISBN 978-1-4765-1407-9 (eBook PDF)
1. Science projects—Juvenile literature. I. Title.
 Q182.3.W45 2013
507.8—dc23   2012030975

Editorial Credits
Mandy Robbins, editor; Tracy McCabe, designer; Marcie Spence, media researcher
Laura Manthe, production specialist

Photo Credits
Capstone Studio: Karon Dubke, 7, (spoons), 9 (hose), 11 (bottom right), 13 (left), 19
(salt & soda), 21 (wrap & vinegar), 24 (pencil & wrap), 28 (newspapers); iStockphoto:
FreezeFrameStudio, 13 (top right), natalie-claude, 12; Shutterstock: 4Max, 14 (hand),
Albo003, 28 (gloves), Aleksey Oleynikov, cover (design element), andersphoto, cover
(microscope), Artsem Martysiuk, (design element), Atovot, 4, 22, 25, Bragin Alexey,
29 (foil), Coprid, 19 (container), Danny Smythe, 6, 15 (measure cup), Dusty Cline,
28 (worms), Edoma, 17 (scissors), 28 (scissors), Elnur, cover (glasses), Emanuela
Grigoras, 24 (spray bottle), Emin Ozkan, 27 (tomato), Feng Yu, 7 (cups), Fpoint, 17
(tape), fredredhat, 16, harveylaw, 20, HelleM, 18 (fish), HSNphotography, 15 (clock),
ID1974, 19 (paper towel), ifong, 19 (faucet), 21 (faucet), Jacob Kearns, 27 (bottle),
Jakub Krechowicz, 9 (soil), Keerati, 9 (trowel), Kletr, 18 (net), KtD, 15 (number),
LockStockBob, 28 (potato & grapes), M. Unal Ozmen, 13 (top right), Margrit Hirsch,
8, 9, (left), Marilyn Volan, (design element), Mark Herreid, 27 (banana), mashe, 26,
(worms), mextix, 29 (tape), motorolka, 17 (cotton swabs), Nils Z, 24 (paper towel),
Oliver Hoffmann, 24 (gloves), Perig, cover (beaker), 3, photosync, 17 (paper), Picsfive,
10, 11 (cup & bowl), robotb, 28 (marker), Roman Sigaev, 21 (egg), Sergiy Telesh,
14 (background), slavchovr, 15 (bowl), Steve Cukrov, cover (scientist), 5, travis
manley, 11 (polish remover), violetkaipaii, 21 (glass), Vitaly Korovin, 23, vladm,
cover (smoke), vovan, 15 (hand), wawritto, 28 (orange & pear), Yuri Shirokov, cover
(iodine), 17 (iodine)

Printed in the United States of America in Brainerd, Minnesota.
092012   006938BANGS13

Table of Contents

Getting Gross with Science

Hands-on science can be slimy, sloppy, stinky, and gross. Just ask the scientists who study spit. Or check with biologists who inspect the living things that grow in manure. But don't let scientists have all the fun. Make your own disgusting scientific discoveries using common materials from around your home. Be sure to dress for a mess!

Using the Metric System

This book provides two systems of measurement. The first one is the standard system of measurement. The official name for this system is "customary units." It is how people in the United States measure things. Scientists usually use a different measuring system, though. Scientists around the world use the metric measuring system. In these activities, you'll find the metric measurements listed in parentheses.

Safety

To stay safe with these projects, follow a few simple guidelines.

1 Check with an adult before doing any experiments.

2 Read the projects all the way through before starting. Be sure to pay attention to any safety tips.

3 If you use a container to do an experiment, don't reuse it later to hold food.

4 Thoroughly wash your hands after doing any of the activities in this book! Washing hands is the best way to prevent spreading harmful bacteria.

Gather up your supplies and get ready to be grossed out by science!

> bacteria—very small living things that exist all around you and inside you; some bacteria cause disease

PRE-DIG CRACKER

Next time you're feeling too lazy to chew, let your spit get started without you. Slobber up a cracker, and let it soak in a spit bath. When you slip that pre-digested cracker into your mouth, you'll be in for a surprise.

What you need:

a saltine cracker,
two small cups,
two spoons,
spit, water

ESTED

1. Split the saltine cracker in half. Put one half in each cup.

2. Use the spoons to crush the crackers.

3. Collect one spoonful of spit. Pour it over one of the crushed crackers.

4. Using the other spoon, pour one spoonful of water over the other cracker.

5. Stir both mixtures. Be sure to use the separate spoons!

6. Wait 10 minutes.

7. Taste both cracker mixtures.

ICKY EXPLANATION: After tasting both crackers, you'll notice that the cracker soaked in spit tasted sweeter. Water just wets the cracker, but spit kicks off digestion the moment it hits food. One of the main ingredients in spit is called amylase. Amylase takes **starch** and breaks it down into sugars. Saltine crackers are mostly starch. Spit sweetens the cracker by turning that starch into sugar.

starch—a white substance found in foods such as potatoes, bread, and rice

Learn the science behind your favorite bathroom accessory. Get out the toilet plunger, press it into a mud puddle, and pull it up. You'll suck up a load of mud and make a farting sound to boot.

TAKE the

What you need:

a patch of bare dirt, a trowel, water, and a plunger

trowel—a hand tool with a flat, pointed blade

1 Locate a patch of bare dirt that is larger than your plunger. For best results, find a spot that is free of rocks and sand.

2 Dig with the trowel to loosen the dirt at least 6 inches (15 centimeters) deep.

3 Soak the patch with water until you have made a mud puddle.

4 Shove the plunger into the mud puddle as hard as you can, as if you are plunging a toilet.

5 Now pull up. Listen and watch as the mud bubbles and farts.

PLUNGE

ICKY EXPLANATION: A plunger transfers the force of your push into the toilet water to push poop down the plumbing. Plungers work best when there is as little air as possible inside them. That's because air inside a plunger cushions your push. When you push on a plunger, air sometimes bubbles out. When you pull up on a plunger after a hard push, you create a vacuum inside the plunger. That's when air can squeak in. Either way, you get funny noises.

GOB OF GOO

What you need:

safety glasses, a face mask, rubber gloves, a Styrofoam cup, a large glass bowl, pure acetone fingernail polish remover, waxed paper

Watch a Styrofoam cup twist and spin as it melts into a puddle of **acetone** fingernail polish remover. Scoop up the gob of goo, squish it, and mold it. Be careful, though. Acetone is flammable, so keep it away from open flames. Do this project outside so you're not breathing in acetone.

1. Put on safety glasses, face mask, and rubber gloves. The gloves stop the acetone from drying out your skin.

2. Set the cup in the bowl.

3. Fill the cup about one-third full of fingernail polish remover. Watch as the cup collapses.

4. Swirl your fingers around inside the bowl to collect the Styrofoam goo. Squish it, and let it ooze between your fingers.

5. When you're done playing with the melted cup, mold it into a statue. Then lay it on waxed paper. Check back in a few hours, and your creation will have dried.

ICKY EXPLANATION: You can drink water all day out of a Styrofoam cup, and the cup won't dissolve. But acetone is another matter. Styrofoam is made of a plastic called polystyrene. When acetone and polystyrene get together, the molecules of polystyrene break apart and dissolve in the acetone. This experiment doesn't use enough acetone to completely dissolve the polystyrene, so there is some goop leftover. The goop hardens into plastic as it dries.

FOR DISPOSAL: Pour any remaining fingernail polish remover back into its bottle. Let your Styrofoam goop dry. Then see if your local recycling center accepts Styrofoam.

acetone—a chemical that is often used to remove fingernail polish

Here's a riddle for you! What's a solid *and* a liquid and fun all over? Have a blast while you experiment with this mind-boggling goo.

SEMISOLID SLIME!

What you need:

two 16-ounce (454-gram) boxes of cornstarch, a cake pan, 3 cups (720 milliliters) of water, food coloring (optional)

1 First dump both containers of cornstarch into your cake pan.

2 Add 3 cups (720 mL) of water to the starch.

3 Add a few drops of food coloring if you want colored slime. Use your hands to combine the mixture.

4 You want the mixture to be thin enough for your fingers to sink in. But it also must be thick enough so you can punch it, and your fist doesn't sink in. If the mixture is too thick for your fingers to sink in, add a little more water.

5 Have fun playing with your semisolid slime. Squeeze it into a solid ball—then let go, and watch it melt back into liquid. Punch it, and watch your hand bounce back. You can even set the pan on the floor and quickly step on it. Your foot won't sink in!

ICKY EXPLANATION: Mixing cornstarch and water creates a fluid that is like quicksand. Cornstarch is made of a group of atoms that act like a chain of paper clips. In small amounts of water, these chains float very close to each other. When the mixture moves slowly, the chains gradually flow past each other like a liquid. But sometimes the mixture is moved quickly, like when you punch or squeeze it. Then the chains get tangled and can't move. They feel and act like a solid.

 atom—an element in its smallest form

Mix up a batch of fake snot. Then expose it to some dust and dirt. You'll find out it's not as useless as you might think.

A HANDFUL

What you need:

psyllium-based fiber supplement powder, water, a large bowl, very dry dirt

1. Mix 1 teaspoon (5 mL) of fiber supplement and 1 cup (240 mL) of water in a large bowl.

2. Microwave the mixture for five minutes. It will be hot, so let it cool for five more minutes. Then take it outside.

3. Scoop up some "snot" in one hand and some dirt in the other hand.

4. Put your hands next to each other, and blow the dirt toward the fake snot.

5. Try to remove the dirt from the fake snot. Can you do it?

OF SNOT

ICKY EXPLANATION: Snot has an important job. The air you breathe is filled with bits of dust, dirt, and germs. They may be too small to see, but they can still damage your lungs or make you sick. Snot, or mucus, traps those bits of dust and germs. Tiny hairs move the snot to the back of your nose and down your throat. You swallow it instead of breathing it. Then your stomach acid destroys whatever the snot trapped.

 psyllium—a seed that expands when exposed to water

SWEAT

Take a sniff of your sneakers. Your sweaty feet are making a stench! Do your feet really sweat more than the rest of you? Use iodine and paper to make a mini map of your sweat glands and find out.

What you'll need:

a scissors, printer paper, a cotton swab, a few drops of iodine (available with first aid supplies), tape

TEST

1. Cut two 0.5–inch (1.3–cm) squares of printer paper.

2. Dip the cotton swab in the iodine, and use it to paint a spot on your forearm. Make the spot a little bigger than the squares of paper.

3. Paint another iodine patch on the bottom of your foot. Try to avoid the creases.

4. Let the iodine dry completely.

5. Tape a paper square on top of each iodine spot.

6. In 30 minutes, peel off the paper squares.

7. Look for black spots on the paper. Each spot shows one of your sweat glands.

ICKY EXPLANATION: When you think about sweat, you probably think of sweaty feet or armpits. But you actually have sweat glands all over your body. They produce little bits of sweat all the time. When you get hot, they make even more sweat. The sweat **evaporates**, cooling your body. In this activity, your sweat moistens the iodine on your skin. The iodine turns black when it hits the starch in the printer paper. You probably noticed that your feet have a lot more sweat glands than your arm. Feet and hands have the most sweat glands of any body part.

→ **iodine**—a brown chemical that turns black when it mixes with starch
gland—an organ that produces chemicals or allows substances to leave the body
evaporate—to change from a liquid into a vapor or a gas

FISH MUMMY

Buy a fresh fish, and prepare it for eternity ancient Egyptian-style. Pack it in salt and baking soda to create a mummified fish. You'll need an adult to help you with some of the steps in this project.

What you need:

a fresh fish (not previously frozen), paper towels, a large bowl, a 1-pound (454-g) box of baking soda, a 26-ounce (737-g) package of salt, a plastic container (large enough to hold the fish) with a lid

1 Have an adult clean and **gut** the fish. Leave the head attached.

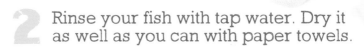

2 Rinse your fish with tap water. Dry it as well as you can with paper towels.

3 In the large bowl, mix the baking soda and salt.

4 Cover the bottom of the plastic container with 2 inches (5 cm) of the salt and baking soda mixture.

5 Stuff the body cavity of the fish with more of the mixture.

6 Lay the fish in the container. Dump the rest of the mixture on the fish, and close the lid. Leave it sit, unrefrigerated, for one week.

7 After a week, dump out the salt and baking soda and throw it away. If the fish is not completely dry, you will need to repeat the process with fresh salt and baking soda.

ICKY EXPLANATION: A fish is mostly water. When bacteria move in and start the rotting process, they use that water. To stop the fish from rotting, you need to get all of the water out. Gutting the fish removes a lot of water. The salt dries out the rest of the body. Water moves from places that are rich in water to places that have less water in a process called **osmosis**. By packing the fish in salt, you create a very dry place outside of the fish. The water moves into that dry place. The ancient Egyptians used a different salt mixture to draw the water out of dead bodies, but baking soda and table salt work just as well.

FOR DISPOSAL: Your mummified fish can be thrown in the trash.

gut—to remove the inside organs of an animal

osmosis—when fluid moves from an area of high concentration to low concentration through thin tissues that only allow small molecules, such as water, through

EGGS-TRA GROSS BOUNCING BALL

Use vinegar to dissolve the shell from a raw egg. Play with the slimy naked egg. You can even bounce it.

a raw egg, a glass, vinegar, plastic wrap

1 Place the raw egg in the glass.

2 Fill the glass with enough vinegar to cover the egg.

3 Cover the glass with plastic wrap, and let it sit for 24 hours.

4 After a full day of soaking, gently remove the egg from the vinegar. It will be covered with gooey eggshell remains. Rinse them off with cold water.

5 To bounce the egg, drop it from a few inches above a smooth surface. Just don't let it touch anything sharp. If you do, it will pop like a balloon and send stinky raw egg squirting everywhere!

ICKY EXPLANATION: Vinegar is an acid. It's not strong enough to hurt you, but it is strong enough to dissolve an eggshell. Eggshells are made of a chemical called calcium carbonate. When calcium carbonate is put in an acid, a **chemical reaction** takes place. This reaction makes a gas called carbon dioxide. You may see bubbles on the outside of the egg while it soaks. Carbon dioxide is the gas inside those bubbles. Once the eggshell dissolves, a cell membrane is the only thing surrounding the egg's interior. This membrane is tough, but flexible. So you can squeeze it a little, or bounce it from a few inches up.

FOR DISPOSAL: Vinegar can be washed down the sink drain. The egg will have a strong smell, so you will want to dispose of it in an outdoor garbage can.

chemical reaction—a process in which one or more substances are made into a new substance or substances

A POOP WHAT'S WHAT

rubber gloves, droppings from a plant-eating animal, large plastic container, paper towels, a spray bottle full of water, plastic wrap, a pencil

Are you ready to start a garden? Try a manure garden! For this experiment, do not use poop from a cat, dog, mouse, or any other animal that eats meat. These animals may have diseases that can spread to humans. In general, long tubular poop is more likely to be from a cat or dog. Little circles of poop are more likely to be from plant eaters such as deer or rabbits. Big piles of poop often belong to a cow or horse.

1 Put on the rubber gloves. Collect a pile of droppings from a cow, deer, rabbit, horse, or other plant-eater that lives outside.

2 Line your plastic container with three layers of paper towels. Place the poop on top of the paper towels.

3 Spray water on the poop until both the poop and paper towels are wet.

4 Cover the container with plastic wrap. Punch six holes in the plastic wrap with the pencil to allow air in.

5 Place the container in a sunny place.

6 Keep an eye on your "garden" for the next week. If it starts to dry out, pull back the plastic wrap. Spray more water on top, and then cover it back up.

7 In about one week, the first **fungi** should pop up. New fungi will grow every few days for about three weeks.

ICKY EXPLANATION: What do fungi eat for breakfast? Poop! The fungi growing in your container are actually digesting the poop. The garden changes because some types of fungi grow well in fresh manure, but other types need older manure. These fungi have a seriously gross life. They grow in manure and then produce **spores** that spread to nearby grass. When another animal eats the grass, the spores go through the animal and come out in the poop. More fungi grow from the pooped-out spores. If you're lucky, you'll see tiny black spots on the plastic wrap that covers your garden. These are the spores from a fungus that spits its spores out of the manure into fresh grass. If you take off the plastic wrap, they might even spit in your face. Don't worry, though. As long as you aren't made of cow manure, the spores can't grow on you.

FOR DISPOSAL: Manure from vegetable eaters makes great fertilizer. Spread your project leftovers in an outdoor garden or bury it.

fungi—organisms that have no leaves, flowers, or roots; mushrooms and molds are fungi

spore—a plant cell that develops into a new plant; spores are produced by plants that do not flower, such as fungi, mosses, and ferns

WORM

What you need:

a marker,
an empty 2-liter bottle,
scissors, four sheets of
newspaper, rubber gloves, food
waste (that does not include
meat, oil, or dairy products),
a large bowl, water, composting
worms (such as red wrigglers),
clear packing tape,
aluminum foil

POOP

Rotten tomatoes. Old fingernail clippings. Slimy black bananas. Worms love them all! Have an adult help you make them a cozy home in a bottle. Dump in your garbage, and watch your waste transform into rich fertilizer.

1 Draw a line around the bottle about 2 inches (5 cm) from the top of the bottle. Have an adult help you cut around the line. Save the top of the bottle.

2 Cut the newspaper into 1.5-inch (4-cm) strips. Then cut them the other direction to make 1.5-inch (4-cm) squares.

3 Put on your rubber gloves. Gather about 2 cups (480 mL) of food waste that does not include any meat, oils, or dairy. You can also include fingernail clippings and hair from a hair brush.

4 Mix the waste and newspaper clippings in the large bowl by hand. Add water until the mixture is wet but not dripping. Put it in the bottle.

5 Add about 50 composting worms, such as red wrigglers. You can buy them online or from a bait shop. (The type of earthworms you dig from the dirt will not work.)

6 Use clear packing tape to tape the top of the bottle back on.

7 Cover the bottle with aluminum foil. Leave the cap off to let a little air in between the foil and the plastic. You will be able to peel back the aluminum foil to see the worms at work.

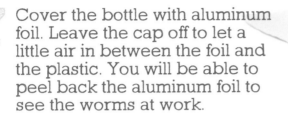

ICKY EXPLANATION: Worms love what we waste. They suck up the garbage through a tiny mouth at one end of their bodies. The garbage then travels to the **gizzard**. Since worms don't have teeth, their gizzard is full of sand and grit to grind up the food. Bits of old banana peels or fingernails then slide down the intestines and come out as little black wads. Scientists call them castings. You'll be able to see these castings on the wall of your bottle. After two or three months, the worms will have digested most of your food. At that point, you can open the bottle and mix in more garbage. Or you can mix the compost into your garden to improve the soil.

FOR DISPOSAL: There's no need to dispose of this project. Composting is always a great idea. If you decide you're through with it, find a friend who composts. They will love to get a free starter kit.

 gizzard—the part of a worm's stomach that is used for crushing food

Glossary

acetone (AS-uh-tone)—a toxic chemical used to remove hard enamels such as nail polish, car paints, and strong glues

atom (AT-uhm)—an element in its smallest form

bacteria (bak-TEER-ee-uh)—very small living things that exist all around you and inside you; some bacteria cause disease

chemical reaction (KE-muh-kuhl ree-AK-shuhn)—a process in which one or more substances are made into a new substance or substances

evaporate (i-VA-puh-rayt)—to change from a liquid into a vapor or a gas

fungi (FUHN-jy)—organisms that have no leaves, flowers, or roots

gizzard (GIH-zurd)—the part of a worm's stomach that is used for crushing food

gland (GLAND)—an organ that produces chemicals or allows substances to leave the body

gut (GUHT)—to remove the inside organs of an animal

iodine (EYE-uh-dine)—a chemical element that is used to kill germs

osmosis (oz-MOH-siss)—when fluid moves from an area of high concentration to low concentration through thin tissues that only allow small molecules through

psyllium (SIL-ee-um)—a seed that expands when exposed to water

spore (SPOR)—a plant cell that develops into a new plant

starch (STARCH)—a white substance found in foods such as potatoes, bread, and rice

trowel (TROU-uhl)—a hand tool with a flat blade

Read More

Davids, Stacy B. *Strange but True Science.* Strange but True. Mankato, Minn.: Capstone Press, 2011.

Harris, Elizabeth Snoke. *Yikes! Wow! Yuck!: Fun Experiments for Your First Science Fair.* New York: Lark Books, 2008.

Wheeler-Toppen, Jodi. *Science Experiments That Fizz and Bubble: Fun Projects for Curious Kids.* Kitchen Science. Mankato, Minn.: Capstone Press, 2011.

Internet Sites

FactHound offers a safe, fun way to find Internet sites related to this book. All of the sites on FactHound have been researched by our staff.

Here's all you do:

Visit *www.facthound.com*

Type in this code: 9781429699242

Check out projects, games and lots more at
www.capstonekids.com

Index